HOW TO

EASTER AND 101 CUTE STUFF

How To Use This Book

- Prepare A Pencil And Eraser, You Can Use Pens Or Marke Or Any Tool You Like.

- Start By Drawing Lightly So That It Can Be Easily Erased If There Are Mistakes.

- Continue By Following The Arrow Step.

- If You Ever Get Stuck On Drawing You Can Always Look At The Final Drawing.

- After Completed A Drawing You Can be Coloring It In Any Way You Like.

What's Inside

DUCK OR RABBIT ?

What's Inside

DUCK OR RABBIT ?

PRACTIC

BUNNY

PRACTIC

BUNNY EGG

PRACTIC

BUNNY

PRACTIC

BUNNY

CHICKEN

PRACTIC

EGG

PRACTIC

BUNNY

PRACTIC

BUNNY

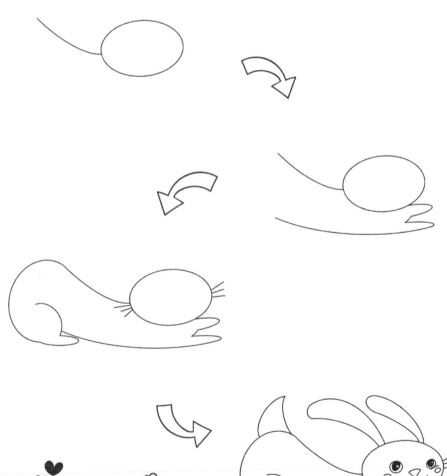

RABBIT

CHICKS

START

PRACTIC

PENGUIN

START

PRACTIC

CLOUD

START

PRACTIC

NARWHAL

START

PRACTIC

CUPCAKE

START

PRACTICE

DANGO

START

PRACTIC

WATERMELON

START

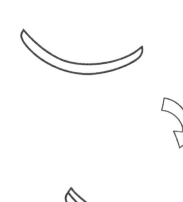

PRACTIC

HOT AIR BALLOON

START

PRACTIC

BOAT

START

PRACTIC

WORLD

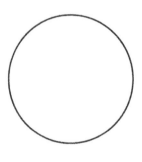

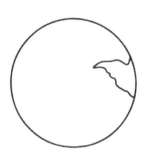

FIRE

START

PRACTIC

MARKER

START

PRACTIC

PHONE

START

PRACTIC

SHAMPOO

START

PRACTIC

OWL

START

PRACTIC

SCREWDRIVER

START

PRACTIC

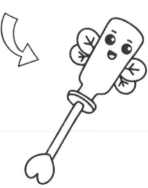

PLIERS

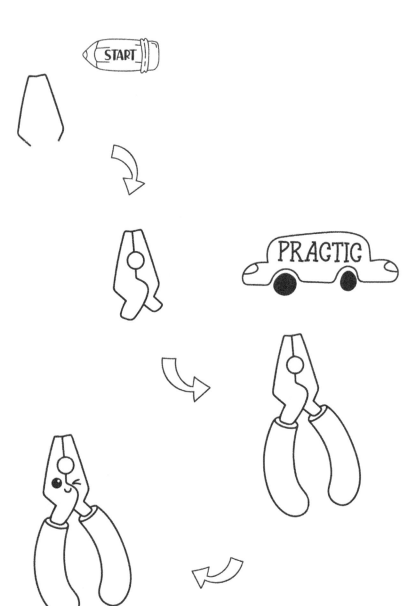

START

PRACTIC

CLOCK

START

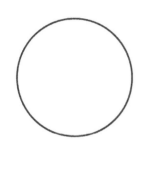

PRACTIC

HAMMER

PRACTIC

SOAP

START

PRACTIC

PLANE

START

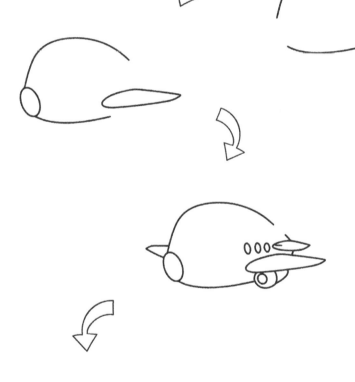

PRACTIC

FISH

START

PRACTIC

DRILL

START

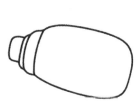

PRACTIC

PIG

START

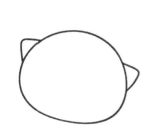

PRACTIC

SHEEP

START

PRACTIC

GIRAFFE

START

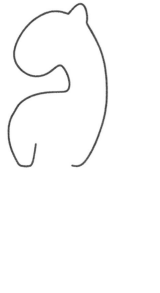

PRACTICE

CARROT

START

PRACTIC

FACE WASH

START

PRACTIC

LIPSTICK

 START

PRACTIC

BOOK

START

PRACTIC

OCTOPUS

START

PRACTIC

PENGUIN

START

PRACTIC

CACTUS

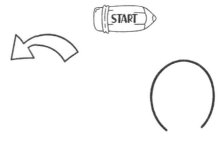

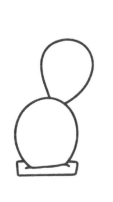

PRACTICE

TEA BAG

PRACTIC

SPACESHIP

START

PRACTIC

PLATYPUS

START

PRACTIC

START

PRACTIC

ERASER

START

PRACTIC

CANDY

START

Practice

KOALA

START

PRACTIC

RAINBOW

MILK BOX

START

BEE

START

FRENCH FRIES

START

PRACTIC

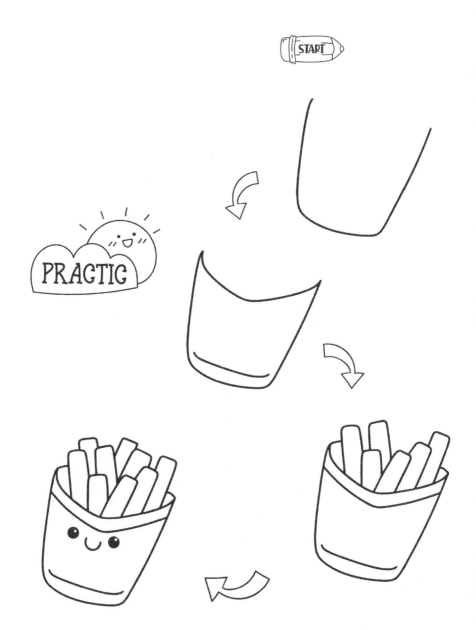

POTION BOTTLES

 START

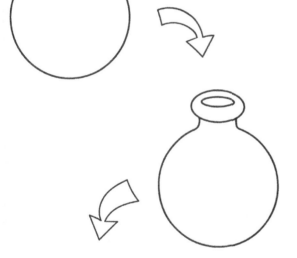

PRACTIC

BURGER

START

❤ PRACTIC ❤

SCISSORS

START

PRACTIC

GUITAR

START

PRACTIC

STAPLER

PRACTIC

BATHTUB

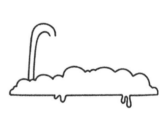

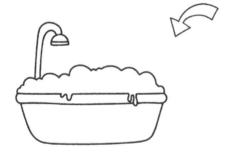

PRACTIC

START

PRACTIC

BACKPACK

START

PRACTIC

SEAHORSE

START

PRACTIC

HAIR DRYER

START

PRACTIC

TROPHY

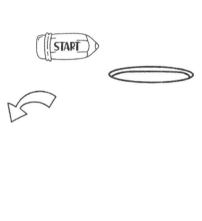

PRACTIC

#1 DAD

PINEAPPLE

START

CANDLE

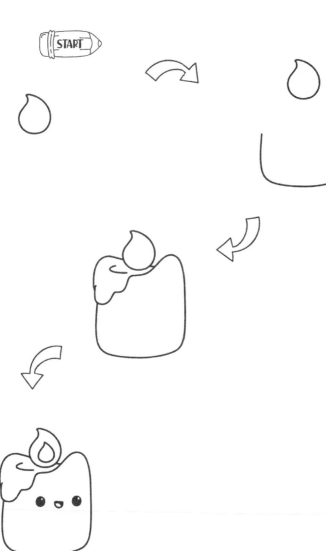

START

PRACTIC

SLOTH

START

MUSHROOM

START

PRACTIC

MERMAID TAIL

START

PRACTIC

MUG

PRACTIC

SANDWICH

START

PRACTIC

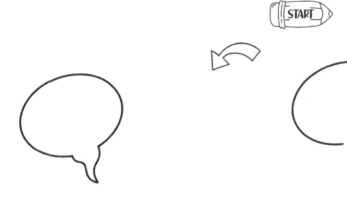

CUPCAKE

START

PRACTIC

START

PRACTIC

WALLET

START

PRACTIC

CINNABON

START

PRACTIC

BREAD

START

PRACTIC

PIZZA

START

PRACTIC

CORN

START

PRACTIC

ICE CREAM

START

PRACTICE

CAT

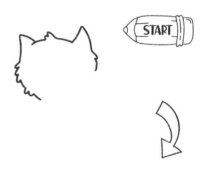

PRACTIC

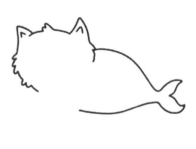

ROCK

START

PRACTIC

PEACH

TURTLES

START

PRACTIC

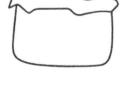

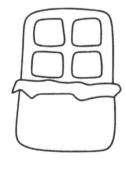

PEAR

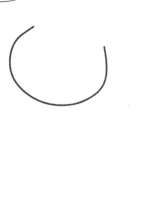

PRACTIC

TOILET PAPER

PRACTIC

SQUID

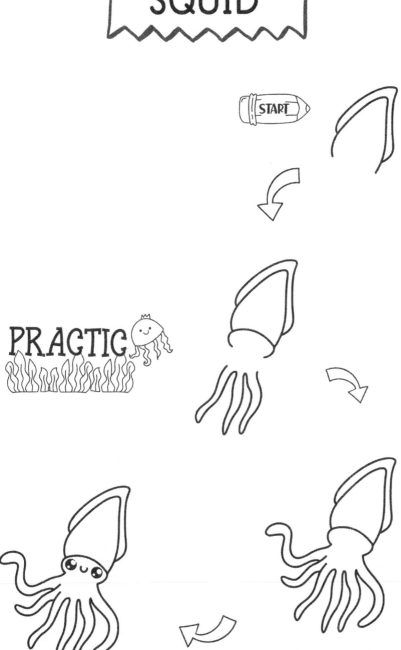

START

PRACTICE

FLOWER

START

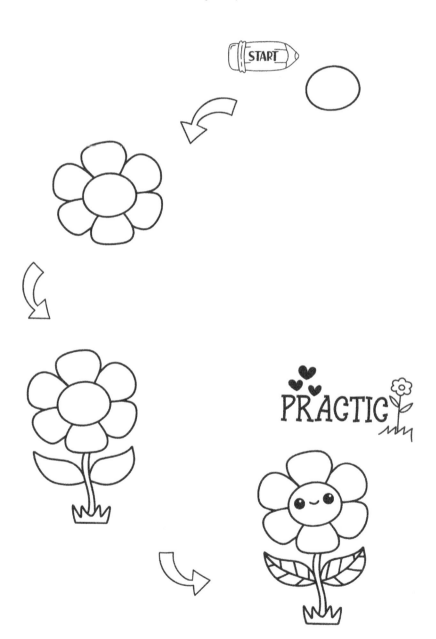

PRACTICE

GHOST

START

JUICE

BIRD

START

PRACTIC

SNAIL

START

PRACTIC

SUSHI

START

PRACTIC

CHERRY

START

PRACTIC

HAMSTER

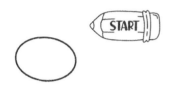

 PRACTIC

UMBRELLA

START

PRACTIC

JELLO

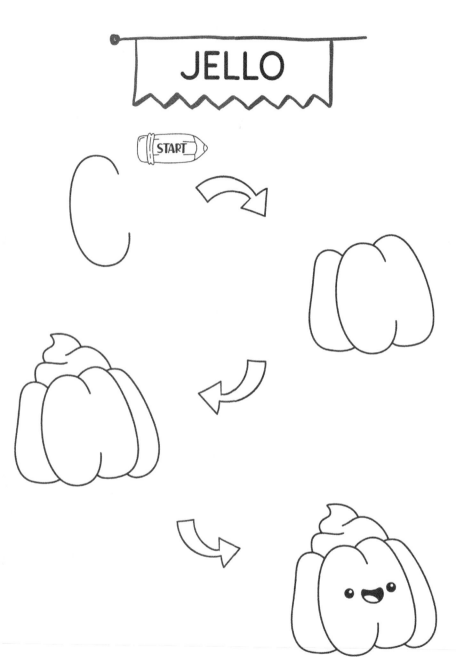

START

PRACTIC

DINOSAUR

DONUT

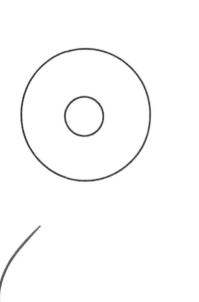 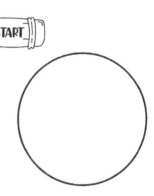

 PRACTIC

BUTTERFLY

START

POPCORN

START

PRACTIC

ALOE VERA

PRACTICE

AVOCADO

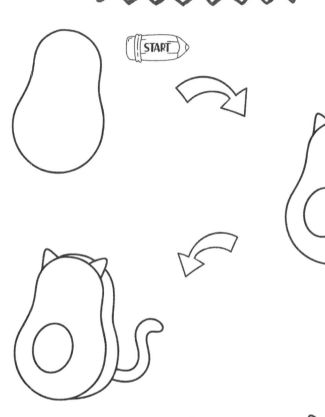

START

PRACTIC

ELEPHANT

START

PRACTIC

BANANA

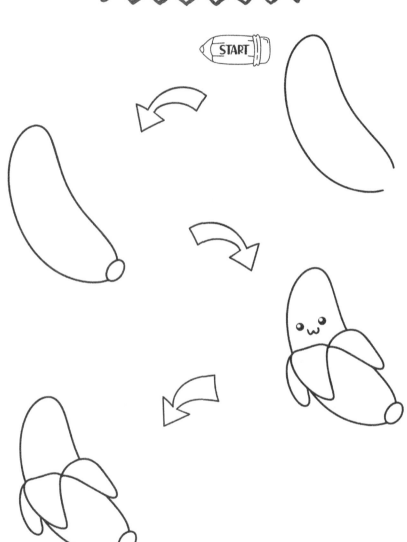

START

PRACTIC

AXOLOTL

START

PRACTICE

Made in the USA
Monee, IL
05 April 2023

31352507R00066